Created and published by Knock Knock
Distributed by Who's There Inc.
Venice, CA 90291
knockknockstuff.com

Illustrations by Dana Svobodovà

This book is a work of humor meant solely for entertainment purposes. Filling out and/or failing
to fill out the lists may lead to a life of chronic laziness or, perhaps, a profound sense of relief and
satisfaction. It's your call, really. The publisher and anyone associated with the production of this
book do not advocate breaking the law. In no event will Knock Knock be liable to any reader for
any damages, including direct, indirect, incidental, special, consequential, or punitive arising out
of or in connection with the use of the lines contained in this book. And that's that.

ISBN: 978-160106583-4
UPC: 825703-50067-7

10 9 8 7 6 5 4 3 2 1

IT'S A SIMPLE, UNIVERSAL FACT: WE LIVE, WE DIE, AND IN BETWEEN THERE'S ALL KINDS OF STUFF WE DON'T DO THAT WE WISH WE COULD.

After all, life is short, and there's lots of TV to watch and laundry to fold while you're feeling guilty for not having climbed Mount Kilimanjaro . . . yet.

And so, to assuage our guilt we make a list—a bucket list—of things we wish to do before we die or else we will have lived our lives in vain. Such panic-induced, fantasy list-making behavior has a name: delusion. In a high-pressure world of must-haves and need-to-dos, it's only sensible to give yourself the gift of managed expectations. It's time to get real and cross off the things you'll never really do.

You know you're never actually going to bike across the country, so why not spend that desire and sense of inadequacy on something manageable, like walking around the block? Take a break, take a breath, and find something better to do—something that you'll actually do.

Some may consider making a list of things you'll never accomplish counterproductive. But while those people are frantically figuring out how to scrape up the money to buy a ticket to Katmandu, you will have already found inner peace in the comfort of your own home.

TELL THE BUCKET TO BITE IT.

Fig. 1 The Great Wall of China

The Great Wall of China can be seen from space.
You'll never travel to space either.

MONUMENTS
I'LL NEVER VISIT

At Least You Can Read about It

Inhabited since prehistoric times, Petra is a city in Jordan that consists of ornate Greco-Roman buildings carved directly into the pink sandstone mountains. It's astonishingly gorgeous, almost like a film set brought to life. Frequently chosen by well-traveled types as a place you must see before you die, you can be happy just looking up pictures of Petra on the Internet.

Something You Can Actually Do

Once upon a time, cathedral spires were always the tallest, grandest structures around. Now, thanks to elevators, steel, and real estate developers, finding a tall building is easier than ever. Why not take a ride up to the top floor of that nearby office tower as a modern, no-stairs nod to the monuments?

1. _____
2. _____
3. _____
4. _____
5. _____
6. _____
7. *Petra* _____
8. _____
9. _____
10. _____

☐ Chucked It

ROAD TRIPS
I'LL NEVER GO ON

1. _____

2. _____

3. _____

4. _____

5. *Pan-American Highway*

6. _____

7. _____

8. _____

9. _____

10. _____

☐ Chucked It

ATHLETIC EVENTS
I'LL NEVER COMPETE IN

1. _____
2. _____
3. _____
4. _____
5. _____
6. _____
7. _____
8. *Ironman* _____
9. _____
10. _____

☐ Chucked It

VEGETABLES
I'LL NEVER LIKE

1. _____

2. _____

3. _____

4. *Boiled peas* _____

5. _____

6. _____

7. _____

8. _____

9. _____

10. _____

☐ Chucked It

WORLD RECORDS
I'LL NEVER BREAK

1. _____

2. _____

3. _____

4. _____

5. _____

6. _____

7. *Most push-ups* _____

8. _____

9. _____

10. _____

☐ Chucked It

Fig. 2 Flock of Seagulls Hairdo

Get one and it'll be the only thing
anyone will ever remember you for.

HAIRSTYLES
I'LL NEVER SPORT

At Least You Can Read about It

Consider the mullet: Is it an elegant solution to the age-old question "Cut it or grow it"? Or is it a hairstyle with its roots in indecision, an attempt to combine the ease of short hair with the versatility of long? Perhaps the 'do best explained by the phrase "business in front, party in the back" just reflects a fear of commitment. But you'll never know, will you?

Something You Can Actually Do

No matter how much money you spend on that haircut, it's still going to grow out—and grow out fast. It's easy to stay stylish, even with an unruly mane, by wearing a hat. The right hat flatters the face, provides shade, and is a noteworthy accessory to any outfit.

1. _____
2. _____
3. _____
4. _____
5. _____
6. *Mullet* _____
7. _____
8. _____
9. _____
10. _____

☐ Chucked It

TRICKS
I'LL NEVER GET MY DOG TO DO

1. _____
2. _____
3. _____
4. _____
5. _____
6. _____
7. _____
8. *Speak* _____
9. _____
10. _____

☐ Chucked It

WORDS
I'LL NEVER PRONOUNCE CORRECTLY

1. _____
2. _____
3. *Espresso* _____
4. _____
5. _____
6. _____
7. _____
8. _____
9. _____
10. _____

☐ Chucked It

FESTIVALS
I'LL NEVER ATTEND

1. _____
2. _____
3. _____
4. _Running of the bulls_
5. _____
6. _____
7. _____
8. _____
9. _____
10. _____

☐ Chucked It

DIETS
I'LL NEVER GO ON

1. _____
2. _____
3. _____
4. _____
5. _____
6. _____
7. _____
8. _____
9. *Cabbage soup* _____
10. _____

☐ Chucked It

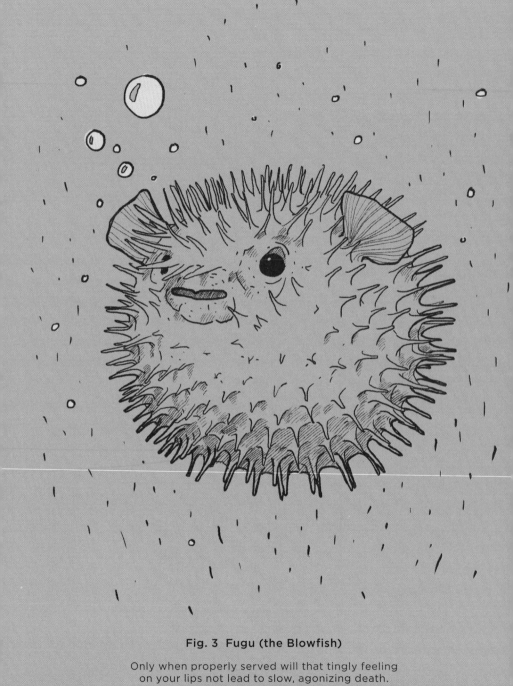

Fig. 3 Fugu (the Blowfish)

Only when properly served will that tingly feeling
on your lips not lead to slow, agonizing death.

FOODS
I'LL NEVER TRY

At Least You Can Read about It

Everything you've heard about haggis is true: Yes, it's a boiled sheep's stomach stuffed with bits of sheep heart, liver, and lungs, and blended with whiskey, animal fat, and oatmeal. Yes, it's the beloved national dish of Scotland, and is often deep-fried. But if you can find a haggis, will you actually eat a haggis? No. No, you won't.

Something You Can Actually Do

If eating adventurously is your cup of tea, but exotic menu items are in scarce supply—look no further than the nearest deli. Few foods contain more esoteric ingredients than a slice of bologna. While some expensive brands are made with only choice cuts of pork and beef, the meat in most commercial bologna comes from such unusual sources as organs and "trimmings."

1. _____

2. _____

3. _____

4. _____

5. _____

6. _____

7. *Haggis* _____

8. _____

9. _____

10. _____

☐ Chucked It

CELEBRITIES
I'LL NEVER SLEEP WITH

1. _____
2. _____
3. _____
4. _____
5. _____
6. *Brangelina* _____
7. _____
8. _____
9. _____
10. _____

☐ Chucked It

SEX ACTS
I'LL NEVER TRY

1. _____
2. _____
3. _____
4. _____
5. _____
6. _____
7. _____
8. *Mile-high club* _____
9. _____
10. _____

☐ Chucked It

BUGS
I'LL NEVER PICK UP IN MY HAND

1. _____

2. _____

3. *Tarantula* _____

4. _____

5. _____

6. _____

7. _____

8. _____

9. _____

10. _____

☐ Chucked It

NATIONAL PARKS
I'LL NEVER VISIT

1. _____
2. _____
3. _____
4. _____
5. *The Everglades* _____
6. _____
7. _____
8. _____
9. _____
10. _____

☐ Chucked It

Fig. 4 The Segway

When *Popular Mechanics* lists reasons why the
Segway isn't that lame anymore—you know you
still don't want to be caught dead riding one.

MODES OF TRANSPORTATION
I'LL NEVER TAKE

At Least You Can Read about It

The Alaskan Itidatrod Race pits teams of sixteen dogs and their human "musher" on a thousand-mile overland course between Nome and Anchorage. Before reliable air flight, dog sled teams were the only way to carry mail across the frozen tundra. And in the icy wilderness, they often mean the only difference between life and death—which is why you'll never find yourself up there.

Something You Can Actually Do

As a slightly less groovy, post roller-disco version of roller skating, rollerblades (aka in-line skates) are equal parts recreation and practical transport. Low impact, easy to learn, and reasonably sidewalk safe, rollerblading is the twenty-first century, utopian ideal of commuting—meaning you can enjoy the sunshine and burn calories (instead of gas) while also getting a few errands done.

1. _____
2. _____
3. _____
4. _____
5. _____
6. _Dogsled_ _____
7. _____
8. _____
9. _____
10. _____

☐ Chucked It

AREAS OF THE HOUSE
I'LL NEVER CLEAN

1. _____
2. _____
3. _____
4. _____
5. _____
6. _____
7. *Behind the stove* _____
8. _____
9. _____
10. _____

☐ Chucked It

COUNTRIES
I'LL NEVER TRAVEL TO

1. _____
2. _____
3. _____
4. _____
5. _Greenland_____
6. _____
7. _____
8. _____
9. _____
10. _____
☐ Chucked It

WORKOUTS
I'LL NEVER ATTEMPT

1. _____
2. _____
3. _____
4. _Hot yoga_____
5. _____
6. _____
7. _____
8. _____
9. _____
10. _____

☐ Chucked It

RISKS
I'LL NEVER TAKE

1. _____

2. _____

3. _____

4. _____

5. _____

6. _____

7. _____

8. *Investing in credit default swaps*

9. _____

10. _____

☐ Chucked It

Fig. 5 The Troll Doll

Ray Dyson of Edmonton, Canada has collected 1,754 troll dolls.
So you might as well just give up now.

COLLECTIONS
I'LL NEVER START

At Least You Can Read about It

Collecting vintage sports cars ranks just below owning a boat as an optimal way to bid farewell to your hard-earned cash. There are plenty of semiaffordable, non-Ferrari fixer-uppers out there to be had. But when you add up the expense of storing and maintaining classic cars in drivable (read: resalable) condition, even a lowly 1979 Pontiac Firebird makes collecting fine art seem like a bargain.

Something You Can Actually Do

Some pop culture appraisers believe the humble compact disc, or CD, may be the next big valuable collectible—especially if the music was only released on CD. The soon-to-be-obsolete media is easy to store and many titles can be bought for pennies at yard sales . . . or found in the back of your closet.

1. _____

2. _____

3. _____

4. _____

5. _____

6. _____

7. _____

8. _____

9. *Vintage sports cars*

10. _____

☐ Chucked It

PHOBIAS
I'LL NEVER OVERCOME

1. _____
2. _____
3. _____
4. _____
5. _____
6. *Fear of dentists (dentophobia)*
7. _____
8. _____
9. _____
10. _____

☐ Chucked It

GREAT BOOKS
I'LL NEVER FINISH

1. _____
2. _____
3. _____
4. *War and Peace*
5. _____
6. _____
7. _____
8. _____
9. _____
10. _____

☐ Chucked It

UNSOLVED CRIMES
I'LL NEVER SOLVE

1. _____

2. _____

3. _____

4. _____

5. _____

6. _____

7. *Jimmy Hoffa's disappearance*

8. _____

9. _____

10. _____

☐ Chucked It

SONGS
I'LL NEVER SING
WITH THE CORRECT LYRICS

1. _____
2. _____
3. _____
4. _____
5. _____
6. _____
7. _____
8. *"Louie, Louie"* _____
9. _____
10. _____

☐ Chucked It

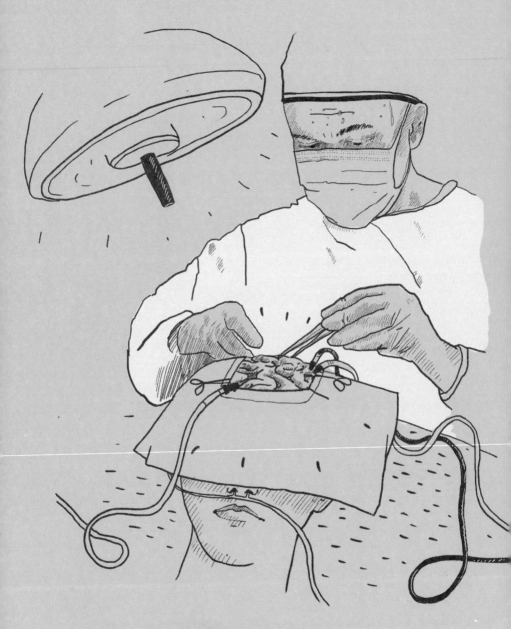

Fig. 6 Brain Surgeon

You'll be on call twenty-four hours a day. And the pressure?
Life-and-death is not a metaphor here.

DREAM JOBS
I'LL NEVER HAVE

At Least You Can Read about It

Aspiring astronauts must be in superb physical condition and hold an advanced degree in engineering, hard science, or math to be considered by NASA. Once that hurdle is cleared, two-plus years of rigorous training are followed by a slew of courses like Russian and robotics. Yet performing brilliantly is no guarantee of blasting off—NASA has severely curtailed the human spaceflight program in recent years.

Something You Can Actually Do

Every successful person gives the same advice to young graduates: do what you love. But what if that means eating ice cream? Or sleeping? There's no better time to start home-based training as a "freelance tester." Which brand of gelato is the creamiest? Is a pillow-top mattress really more comfy? These are the skills that turn ordinary enthusiasts into pros—who then sell their informed opinions on the Internet.

1. _____

2. _____

3. *Astronaut* _____

4. _____

5. _____

6. _____

7. _____

8. _____

9. _____

10. _____

☐ Chucked It

CAUSES
I'LL NEVER GET PASSIONATE ABOUT

1. _____
2. _____
3. _____
4. _____
5. _____
6. _____
7. *Prison reform* _____
8. _____
9. _____
10. _____

☐ Chucked It

SPA TREATMENTS
I'LL NEVER INDULGE IN

1. _____
2. _____
3. _____
4. _____
5. *Four-handed massage* _____
6. _____
7. _____
8. _____
9. _____
10. _____

☐ Chucked It

REBELLIOUS ACTS
I'LL NEVER COMMIT

1. _____
2. _____
3. _____
4. _____
5. _Up and quit_____
6. _____
7. _____
8. _____
9. _____
10. _____

☐ Chucked It

MARTIAL ARTS
I'LL NEVER MASTER

1. _____
2. _____
3. *Krav Maga* _____
4. _____
5. _____
6. _____
7. _____
8. _____
9. _____
10. _____

☐ Chucked It

Fig. 7 Greek

There's a reason they say "It's all Greek to me"—
nobody learns to speak it.

LANGUAGES
I'LL NEVER LEARN

At Least You Can Read about It

The Basque language, or Euskera, is fascinating because it's a "language isolate": it's not related to any other language and linguists aren't quite sure where it comes from. Spoken among the Basque people, most of whom live along the border of France and Spain, it's notable for having lots of consonants, especially X, K, and Z. Fewer than one million people speak it, however, so you won't be missing much.

Something You Can Actually Do

Why learn a complicated, dead language like Latin when in mere minutes you can be fluent in the pseudo-language of Pig Latin? To speak Pig Latin, simply transpose initial consonants to a word's end, followed by –ay (example: "atin-Lay") and add –ay or –way to the ends of words beginning with vowels. Pig Latin's not just for kids or the Three Stooges (amscray!): Shakespeare used an older version of this wordplay in his comedy *Love's Labour's Lost*.

1. _____
2. *Basque* _____
3. _____
4. _____
5. _____
6. _____
7. _____
8. _____
9. _____
10. _____
☐ Chucked It

ADRENALINE RUSHES
I'LL NEVER EXPERIENCE

1. _____
2. _____
3. _____
4. *Base jumping* _____
5. _____
6. _____
7. _____
8. _____
9. _____
10. _____

☐ Chucked It

THINGS
I'LL NEVER TELL MY PARENTS ABOUT

1. _____

2. _____

3. _____

4. _____

5. _____

6. _____

7. _____

8. *That trip to Mexico*

9. _____

10. _____

☐ Chucked It

WORDS
I'LL NEVER LEARN TO SPELL

1. _____
2. _____
3. *Accommodate* _____
4. _____
5. _____
6. _____
7. _____
8. _____
9. _____
10. _____

☐ Chucked It

POETS
I'LL NEVER READ

1. _____

2. _____

3. _____

4. _____

5. _____

6. *Henry Wadsworth Longfellow*

7. _____

8. _____

9. _____

10. _____

☐ Chucked It

Fig. 8 Jim Morrison's Grave

The Lizard King may or may not actually be there.

FAMOUS GRAVESITES
I'LL NEVER VISIT

At Least You Can Read about It

Since his death in 1924, millions of people have visited the embalmed body of the Soviet leader. It's doubtful, however, how many of them would have gone to pay their respects had the state not pressured them to do so. The good news is that today a visit is completely voluntary—and the viewing line is a lot shorter.

Something You Can Actually Do

Victorians made it a common practice to picnic on Sundays among the tombstones of their local graveyards. Whether you're into the gothic or not, it seems they were onto something. Green, shaded, and quiet, many cemeteries are, indeed, designed like parks. Even in the most crowded, urban city, what more peaceful and bucolic spot might you find than the nearest place of eternal rest?

1. _____

2. _____

3. _____

4. _____

5. _____

6. _____

7. *Lenin's Tomb* _____

8. _____

9. _____

10. _____

☐ Chucked It

WRONGS
I'LL NEVER RIGHT

1. _____
2. _____
3. _____
4. _Dumping my ex by text_
5. _____
6. _____
7. _____
8. _____
9. _____
10. _____

☐ Chucked It

GRUDGES
I'LL NEVER GET OVER

1. _____
2. _____
3. _____
4. _____
5. _That jerk at work_____
6. _____
7. _____
8. _____
9. _____
10. _____

☐ Chucked It

CRUSHES
I'LL NEVER ACT UPON

1. _____
2. _____
3. _My shrink_____
4. _____
5. _____
6. _____
7. _____
8. _____
9. _____
10. _____

☐ Chucked It

BEACHES
I'LL NEVER LIE UPON

1. _____
2. _____
3. _____
4. _____
5. _____
6. _____
7. _____
8. _Playa Paraiso (Cuba)_____
9. _____
10. _____

☐ Chucked It

Fig. 9 A Pot-Bellied Pig

For nearly two decades, George Clooney
famously shared his home with Max the potbellied pig.
You're no George Clooney.

PETS
I'LL NEVER HAVE

At Least You Can Read about It

Christian the Lion, a lion cub purchased at the famed London department store Harrods and later returned to the wild by his owners, became a viral video sensation when he was filmed bear-hugging his former keepers after years of separation. Touching, yes. But one man's snuggle with a big cat is your potential near-death experience.

Something You Can Actually Do

With a betta (better known as a Siamese fighting fish) you can get your taste for something wild on a miniscule budget. The colorful, freshwater breed lives a long, solitary life (typically five years) building bubble nests in which to hide. Place a mirror up to one's bowl, however, and its aggressive "rumble fish" nature comes out—puffing out the gills and flashing its lush, iridescent fins.

1. _____
2. _____
3. _____
4. _____
5. _____
6. _____
7. *Lion cub* _____
8. _____
9. _____
10. _____

☐ Chucked It

DANCES
I'LL NEVER DANCE

1. _____
2. _____
3. _____
4. _____
5. *Clogging* _____
6. _____
7. _____
8. _____
9. _____
10. _____

☐ Chucked It

SIGNATURE ITEMS
I'LL NEVER ADD TO MY WARDROBE

1. _____
2. _____
3. *Berets* _____
4. _____
5. _____
6. _____
7. _____
8. _____
9. _____
10. _____

☐ Chucked It

AQUATIC ACTIVITIES
I'LL NEVER ATTEMPT

1. _____
2. _____
3. _____
4. _____
5. _____
6. _____
7. _Pearl diving_____
8. _____
9. _____
10. _____

☐ Chucked It

LOST STUFF
I'LL NEVER FIND

1. _____
2. _____
3. _____
4. *Left sock* _____
5. _____
6. _____
7. _____
8. _____
9. _____
10. _____

☐ Chucked It

Fig. 10 Hands on a Hardbody

It's a cinch to win a pickup truck simply by standing
with your hands on one for several days, right?
Here's a hint: it isn't.

COMPETITIONS
I'LL NEVER ENTER

At Least You Can Read about It

In 2013 at the annual Nathan's Famous Fourth of July International Hot-Dog-Eating Contest, Joey "Jaws" Chestnut won his seventh straight title by consuming sixty-nine hot dogs in ten minutes, and beat his own record set the year before in which he managed a mere sixty-two. Chestnut doesn't restrict himself to hot dogs, however. Among his other feats (according to Major League Eating, the ruling body for these competitions), in 2006 Chestnut ate 118 jalapeño poppers in ten minutes, which is 110 more than common sense would dictate.

Something You Can Actually Do

Rock Paper Scissors—or Rochambo—requires no special equipment or apparatuses, just hands. Form a clenched fist for the rock, keep your hand flat with fingers together to make paper, or extend your index and middle fingers into a "V," peace sign style, for scissors. The rules are simple: Paper covers rock. Rock crushes scissors. Scissors cut paper. Some may argue that strategy is required (there is, after all, now a World Series of RPS), but it's a heck of a lot easier than chess.

1. _____

2. _____

3. _____

4. _____

5. _____

6. _____

7. *Hot-dog-eating contest*

8. _____

9. _____

10. _____

☐ Chucked It

SONGS
I'LL NEVER SING IN PUBLIC

1. _____
2. _____
3. *"Bohemian Rhapsody"*
4. _____
5. _____
6. _____
7. _____
8. _____
9. _____
10. _____

☐ Chucked It

MUSIC
I'LL NEVER APPRECIATE

1. _____
2. _____
3. _____
4. _____
5. _____
6. _____
7. _____
8. _____
9. *A cappella* _____
10. _____

☐ Chucked It

BEVERAGES
THAT WILL NEVER BECOME
MY SIGNATURE DRINK

1. _____
2. _____
3. _____
4. *Shirley Temple* _____
5. _____
6. _____
7. _____
8. _____
9. _____
10. _____

☐ Chucked It

PUZZLES
I'LL NEVER SOLVE

1. _____
2. _____
3. _____
4. _____
5. _____
6. _____
7. _____
8. *Rubik's Cube*
9. _____
10. _____

☐ Chucked It

Fig. 11 Kon-Tiki

Thor Heyerdal's Kon-Tiki expedition is the stuff great films
are made of. Why actually live it when you can watch it
from the comfort of your own living room?

EPIC JOURNEYS
I'LL NEVER UNDERTAKE

At Least You Can Read about It

The Dakar Rally is a rugged 10,000-kilometer road race covering multiple countries that can be completed on a motorcycle, car, or truck. It once ran from France to Senegal, though after security concerns in Mauritania, racers now cover terrain throughout South America. But with an average race running longer than two weeks, who has that kind of vacation time?

Something You Can Actually Do

Cross your nearest state line by foot or car for all of the thrill of an epic journey with only a fraction of the effort. Don't forget to snap a photo of the "Welcome To" sign as a way to commemorate the special moment. If you've got the time, you could visit the last word in border crossings: The Four Corners, the precise spot where the four states of Arizona, Colorado, New Mexico, and Utah touch.

1. _____

2. _____

3. _____

4. _____

5. _____

6. _____

7. _____

8. *Dakar Rally* _____

9. _____

10. _____

☐ Chucked It

STATES
I'LL NEVER DRIVE TO

1. _____
2. _Alaska_____
3. _____
4. _____
5. _____
6. _____
7. _____
8. _____
9. _____
10. _____

☐ Chucked It

ANIMALS
I'LL NEVER MEET IN THE WILD

1. _____
2. _____
3. _____
4. _____
5. *Great white shark* _____
6. _____
7. _____
8. _____
9. _____
10. _____

☐ Chucked It

CROWDS
I'LL NEVER SPEAK IN FRONT OF

1. _____
2. _____
3. _____
4. _____
5. *Nudist convention*
6. _____
7. _____
8. _____
9. _____
10. _____

☐ Chucked It

RECIPES
I'LL NEVER MASTER

1. _____

2. _____

3. *Cheese soufflé* _____

4. _____

5. _____

6. _____

7. _____

8. _____

9. _____

10. _____

☐ Chucked It

Fig. 12 Nail Biting

Nail biting is a crude grooming technique.
But it's cheaper than a manicure.

BAD HABITS
I'LL NEVER QUIT

At Least You Can Read about It

The distractions of the digital age might convince you that procrastination is a modern ill. Yet its biggest sufferer may have been Samuel Johnson, who back in 1751 wrote: "Among all who sacrifice future advantage to present inclination, scarcely any gain so little as those that suffer themselves to freeze in idleness." It took Johnson nine long years to complete the first modern dictionary. Then he died.

Something You Can Actually Do

Staying up late and not getting enough sleep is becoming an all-too-common practice in today's society. So the workaholic in you can rejoice in research showing that taking a quick twenty-minute power nap could help you gain a better memory, sharpen your focus, lose weight, and improve your mood. Just keep in mind that you'll improve your chances of maintaining employment if you snooze in your car instead of at your desk.

1. _____

2. _____

3. _____

4. *Procrastination* _____

5. _____

6. _____

7. _____

8. _____

9. _____

10. _____

☐ Chucked It

GREAT RESTAURANTS
I'LL NEVER DINE AT

1. _____
2. _____
3. _____
4. _____
5. _____
6. _____
7. *Le Jules Verne (Paris, France)*
8. _____
9. _____
10. _____

☐ Chucked It

CAPITALS
I'LL NEVER VISIT

1. _____

2. _____

3. _____

4. *Luxembourg City* _____

5. _____

6. _____

7. _____

8. _____

9. _____

10. _____

☐ Chucked It

HEALTHY HABITS
I'LL NEVER ADOPT

1. _____
2. *Flossing twice a day* _____
3. _____
4. _____
5. _____
6. _____
7. _____
8. _____
9. _____
10. _____

☐ Chucked It

HOBBIES
I'LL NEVER TAKE UP

1. _____
2. _____
3. _____
4. _____
5. _____
6. _____
7. _____
8. _Beekeeping_____
9. _____
10. _____

☐ Chucked It

Fig. 13 Private Jet

The ticket price for the freedom not to pay a baggage fee?
Approximately $8,766.08 per hour.

LUXURY ITEMS
I'LL NEVER AFFORD

At Least You Can Read about It

The Versailles house in Windermere, Florida is timeshare tycoon David Siegel's unfinished 90,000-square-foot palace of opulence. The subject of the 2012 documentary *The Queen of Versailles*, it includes ten kitchens, thirteen bedrooms, a bowling alley, and a twenty-car garage. Building began in 2004, halted in 2008 due to foreclosure, resumed in 2013, and is rumored to be completed by 2016. If a billionaire can't manage to finance such a thing, neither can you.

Something You Can Actually Do

Can't afford caviar? With the price reaching record highs and world supply shrinking fast due to overfishing, virtually no one can. However, that craving for the colorful, briny, pop-in-your-mouth goodness of caviar can be satisfied with a scoop of affordable salmon roe instead. After all, caviar is fish eggs.

1. _____

2. _____

3. _____

4. _____

5. _____

6. _____

7. *Custom-built mansion*

8. _____

9. _____

10. _____
    ☐ Chucked It

ADVANCED DEGREES
I'LL NEVER GET

1. _____
2. _____
3. _____
4. *PhD in Applied Mathematics*
5. _____
6. _____
7. _____
8. _____
9. _____
10. _____

☐ Chucked It

PRESTIGIOUS TITLES
I'LL NEVER EARN

1. _____
2. _____
3. _____
4. _____
5. _____
6. _____
7. *M'Lord* _____
8. _____
9. _____
10. _____

☐ Chucked It

TECHNOLOGY
I'LL NEVER ADOPT

1. _____
2. _____
3. _____
4. *3-D TV* _____
5. _____
6. _____
7. _____
8. _____
9. _____
10. _____

☐ Chucked It

GADGETS
I'LL NEVER BUY

1. _____
2. _____
3. _____
4. _____
5. *SaladShooter®* _____
6. _____
7. _____
8. _____
9. _____
10. _____

☐ Chucked It

Fig. 14 Bigfoot

Bigfoot is out there somewhere. Good luck finding him.

MYTHICAL CREATURES
I'LL NEVER PROVE THE EXISTENCE OF

At Least You Can Read about It

The kirin, an East Asian version of a unicorn with hooves and a single horn on its head, was once among us, declares North Korea's Korean Central News Agency. Archeologists there claim that they've found a lair of the kirin, once ridden by ancient Korean King Tongmyong. Let's just take their word for it.

Something You Can Actually Do

Luckily, Hans Christian Andersen's famous Little Mermaid sculpture stands in Copenhagen harbor, within close view of any tourist. Copies of the celebrated bronze can also be found in several spots around the globe, including Iowa, Michigan, and Romania. Or if you're in Florida, you can spot a manatee, the very real sea creature Spanish conquistadors thought was a mermaid.

1. _____

2. _____

3. _____

4. _____

5. _____

6. _____

7. _____

8. _____

9. *Unicorn* _____

10. _____

☐ Chucked It

DWELLINGS
I'LL NEVER INHABIT

1. _____
2. *Yurt* _____
3. _____
4. _____
5. _____
6. _____
7. _____
8. _____
9. _____
10. _____

☐ Chucked It

HOME UPGRADES
I'LL NEVER MAKE

1. _____
2. _____
3. *Indoor pool* _____
4. _____
5. _____
6. _____
7. _____
8. _____
9. _____
10. _____

☐ Chucked It

OPERAS
I'LL NEVER SIT THROUGH

1. _____

2. _____

3. _Der Ring des Nibelungen_

4. _____

5. _____

6. _____

7. _____

8. _____

9. _____

10. _____

☐ Chucked It

HISTORICAL FACTS
I'LL NEVER GET STRAIGHT

1. _____
2. _____
3. _____
4. _____
5. *When the Civil War started*
6. _____
7. _____
8. _____
9. _____
10. _____
☐ Chucked It

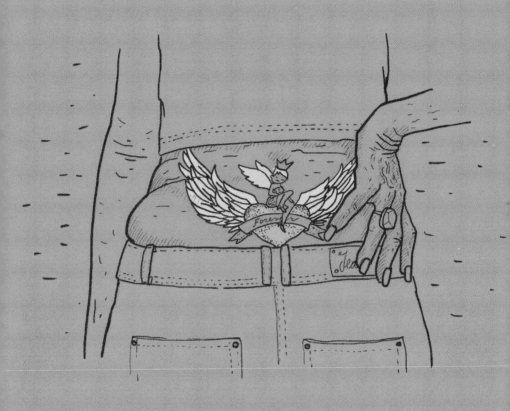

Fig. 15 Lower-Back Tattoo

As if you needed one more reminder
that you're only getting older.

TATTOOS
I'LL NEVER GET

At Least You Can Read about It

In the 1930s and 1940s, Mildred "Millie" Hull was the only female tattoo artist in New York and one of the first to learn the job without the help of a man. Working out of the back of a barbershop (as did many tattooists at the time), she was nicknamed the "Queen of the Bowery." According to *The New Yorker*, the women she inked, including debs and sorority girls, often asked to be marked with their lovers' names. Undoubtedly, Millie would have been twice as busy had she found a way to easily change "Bill" to "Hank."

1. _____

2. _____

3. _____

4. _____

5. _____

6. _____

7. _____

8. *Lover's name* _____

9. _____

10. _____

☐ Chucked It

Something You Can Actually Do

A tattoo is forever—but mehndi, or henna art, is temporary. The leaves from the henna tree, dried and made into a paste, are used for adorning brides (and sometimes grooms) around the world. But you don't have to be celebrating a wedding to partake. Painless, and more importantly, not permanent, this is body art for those who like to try before they buy.

PEOPLE
I'LL NEVER FORGIVE

1. _____
2. _____
3. _____
4. _____
5. *That guy in high school*
6. _____
7. _____
8. _____
9. _____
10. _____

☐ Chucked It

PEOPLE
I'LL NEVER PLEASE

1. _Mom_
2. _Dad_
3.
4.
5.
6.
7.
8.
9.
10.

☐ Chucked It

GREAT WORKS OF ART
I'LL NEVER STAND IN FRONT OF

1. _____
2. _____
3. _____
4. _____
5. *The cave paintings of Lascaux*
6. _____
7. _____
8. _____
9. _____
10. _____

☐ Chucked It

PERIODICALS
TO WHICH I'LL NEVER SUBSCRIBE

1. _____
2. _____
3. *Scientific American* _____
4. _____
5. _____
6. _____
7. _____
8. _____
9. _____
10. _____

☐ Chucked It

Fig. 16 Pottery

You'll put years and years of dirty work
into that lopsided set of cereal bowls.

TALENTS
I'LL NEVER MASTER

At Least You Can Read about It

Only eleven people hold the title of Master Penman. And let's be honest, you're probably not going to be number twelve. Inductees must demonstrate a "distinguished level of excellence" in calligraphic categories like "offhand flourishing" and "engrossing and illumination." One master even carves his own pens. All of that just to earn a certificate—that they must pen themselves.

Something You Can Actually Do

Potholder making is a craft that's both easy and practical. Requiring nothing more than a small metal loom and cotton loops, or just old fabric scraps and a sewing machine, it's an art practiced long ago—like when you were in elementary school. Rediscover it today and consider next year's holiday gifts done!

1. _____
2. _____
3. _____
4. _____
5. _____
6. _____
7. *Calligraphy* _____
8. _____
9. _____
10. _____

☐ Chucked It

FICTIONAL PLACES
I'LL NEVER JOURNEY TO
(EVEN IF I COULD)

1. _____
2. _____
3. _____
4. _____
5. _____
6. _____
7. _____
8. _____
9. *Dante's Inferno*
10. _____

☐ Chucked It

WEAPONS
I'LL NEVER WIELD

1. _____
2. _____
3. _____
4. *Spear* _____
5. _____
6. _____
7. _____
8. _____
9. _____
10. _____

☐ Chucked It

STUFF
I'LL NEVER BELIEVE IN

1. _____
2. _____
3. _____
4. *Ghosts* _____
5. _____
6. _____
7. _____
8. _____
9. _____
10. _____

☐ Chucked It

FILMS
I'LL NEVER WATCH

1. _____
2. _____
3. _____
4. _____
5. _____
6. _____
7. _____
8. *Lawrence of Arabia*
9. _____
10. _____

☐ Chucked It

Fig. 17 Cricket

All you need for a quick game of cricket is
twenty-one friends with seventy-two hours to kill.

SPORTS
I'LL NEVER PLAY

At Least You Can Read about It

Embodying the English "cult of manliness" of the 1800s, the objective of rugby football is to carry a ball across the goal line while avoiding over a dozen others intent on knocking the stuffing out of you. Players wear cleats and eschew protective pads or headgear. A battle for the ball is called a "maul." Needless to say, severe injuries are common.

Something You Can Actually Do

Played indoors, and often with a beverage in hand, darts is a game the whole family can enjoy, grumpy uncle included. If you can add, and are capable of tossing small, feathered missiles at a corkboard from 7 feet 9¼ inches away, you're well on your way to becoming a master dart player.

1. _____
2. _____
3. _____
4. _____
5. _____
6. _____
7. *Rugby* _____
8. _____
9. _____
10. _____

☐ Chucked It

CITIES
I'LL NEVER LIVE IN

1. _____
2. _____
3. *Shangri-La* _____
4. _____
5. _____
6. _____
7. _____
8. _____
9. _____
10. _____

☐ Chucked It

BODIES OF WATER
I'LL NEVER SWIM IN

1. _____
2. _____
3. _____
4. _____
5. _____
6. *English Channel*
7. _____
8. _____
9. _____
10. _____

☐ Chucked It

THINGS
I'LL NEVER GET REPAIRED

1. _____
2. _____
3. _____
4. _____
5. _____
6. _____
7. _____
8. *That dent in the bumper*
9. _____
10. _____

☐ Chucked It

WORDS
I'LL NEVER KNOW THE DEFINITION OF

1. _____
2. _____
3. _Sesquipedalian_ _____
4. _____
5. _____
6. _____
7. _____
8. _____
9. _____
10. _____

☐ Chucked It

Fig. 18 Olympic Gold Medal in Weightlifting

He's been training for this moment since he was, like, five years old.
If he's lucky, he'll win a bronze.

AWARDS
I'LL NEVER WIN

At Least You Can Read about It

Awarded for excellence in journalism and the arts since 1917, the Pulitzer Prize is one of the most prestigious awards one can earn, but good luck actually getting it. Even if you could write a widely acclaimed best seller, that's no guarantee of nomination; the Pulitzer committee has long been criticized for overlooking worthy candidates.

Something You Can Actually Do

The Internet is chock-full of sites from which you can customize, download, and print professional-looking personalized award certificates. How about a "Certificate of Achievement" or a "Distinguished Service" award? The titles may seem vague and the accomplishments unspecified, but add a gold seal sticker, put it in a nice frame, hang it on your cubicle wall, and voilà—respect is yours. It may be unearned, but you still get an A for effort.

1. _____
2. _____
3. *The Pulitzer Prize*
4. _____
5. _____
6. _____
7. _____
8. _____
9. _____
10. _____

☐ Chucked It

THINGS
WHOSE POPULARITY
I'LL NEVER UNDERSTAND

1. _____
2. _____
3. _____
4. _____
5. _____
6. _____
7. *Cat videos* _____
8. _____
9. _____
10. _____

☐ Chucked It

BRIDGES
I'LL NEVER CROSS

1. _____

2. _____

3. _____

4. *Bridge on the River Kwai*

5. _____

6. _____

7. _____

8. _____

9. _____

10. _____

☐ Chucked It

HONEYMOON SPOTS
I'LL NEVER TRAVEL TO

1. _____
2. _____
3. _____
4. *Bora Bora* _____
5. _____
6. _____
7. _____
8. _____
9. _____
10. _____

☐ Chucked It

MUSEUMS
I'LL NEVER VISIT

1. _____
2. _____
3. _____
4. _____
5. _____
6. _____
7. *Paris Sewer Museum*
8. _____
9. _____
10. _____

☐ Chucked It

Fig. 19 Hamburger Hall of Fame

The so-called "Home of the Hamburger" is in Seymour, Wisconsin.
Wouldn't you rather just grill one up right now?

HALLS OF FAME
I'LL NEVER VISIT

At Least You Can Read about It

Despite Congress having pronounced jazz as an official American National Treasure, there is no one single Hall of Fame for this acclaimed art form. Alabama, for instance, claims a hall to honor its own jazz legends, as does Oklahoma. With so many states, cities, and publications getting into the act, visiting all of them would be exhausting—and somewhat unnecessary considering so much smooth jazz can be heard in your nearest elevator.

Something You Can Actually Do

Why get bogged down in the endless rancor over who—or what—deserves to be in any given hall of fame when you can start one of your very own? Take inspiration from Tim Arnold. His Pinball Hall of Fame started as a joke (and, perhaps, as a way to store his collection of nearly 1,000 machines), but now is a must-visit for pinball wizards who make their way to Las Vegas, Nevada.

1. _____

2. _____

3. *Jazz Hall of Fame*

4. _____

5. _____

6. _____

7. _____

8. _____

9. _____

10. _____

☐ Chucked It

CARS
I'LL NEVER OWN

1. _____
2. _____
3. _____
4. *James Bond's Aston Martin*
5. _____
6. _____
7. _____
8. _____
9. _____
10. _____

☐ Chucked It

DRUGS
I'LL NEVER TRY

1. _____

2. _____

3. _____

4. _____

5. _____

6. *Opium* _____

7. _____

8. _____

9. _____

10. _____

☐ Chucked It

SPORTING EVENTS
I'LL NEVER ATTEND

1. _____
2. _____
3. _____
4. _____
5. _____
6. _____
7. *Super Bowl* _____
8. _____
9. _____
10. _____

☐ Chucked It

TROPICAL ISLANDS
I'LL NEVER FLY TO

1. _____
2. _____
3. _____
4. *Madagascar* _____
5. _____
6. _____
7. _____
8. _____
9. _____
10. _____

☐ Chucked It

Fig. 20 Harp

You can postpone some activities until after you're dead.

INSTRUMENTS
I'LL NEVER PLAY

At Least You Can Read about It

Invented in 1920 by Russian scientist Leon Theremin, the theremin is an early electronic musical instrument designed to be played completely hands-free—but that doesn't make it easy to master. By moving one's hands carefully inside the instrument's electric field, the player can control frequency and volume of the eerie, humming sound most famously heard in the Beach Boys' "Good Vibrations."

Something You Can Actually Do

The cowbell is very manageable musical instrument. Commonly used in Latin music, it's named after the bells herdsmen place on the necks of their cows to keep track of them. Clapperless cowbells can be found in most any music shop, and are made without that thingie hanging inside to make it clang. It's an idiophone instrument, meaning all you have to do to is hit it with a stick.

1. _____

2. _____

3. _The theremin_____

4. _____

5. _____

6. _____

7. _____

8. _____

9. _____

10. _____

☐ Chucked It

BANDS
I'LL NEVER SEE

1. _____
2. _____
3. _____
4. _____
5. _____
6. _The Beatles_____
7. _____
8. _____
9. _____
10. _____

☐ Chucked It

RELATIVES
I'LL NEVER VISIT

1. _____
2. _____
3. *My second cousins* _____
4. _____
5. _____
6. _____
7. _____
8. _____
9. _____
10. _____
   ☐ Chucked It

HISTORIC SITES
I'LL NEVER VISIT

1. _____
2. _____
3. _____
4. _____
5. _____
6. _____
7. *Leaning Tower of Pisa*
8. _____
9. _____
10. _____

☐ Chucked It

MOUNTAINS
I'LL NEVER CLIMB

1. _____
2. _____
3. _____
4. _____
5. _____
6. _____
7. _____
8. _____
9. _____
10. *Mount Everest*

☐ Chucked It

(Fill in the blank with your own topic.)

1. _____
2. _____
3. _____
4. _____
5. _____
6. _____
7. _____
8. _____
9. _____
10. _____

☐ Chucked It

(Fill in the blank with your own topic.)

1. _____

2. _____

3. _____

4. _____

5. _____

6. _____

7. _____

8. _____

9. _____

10. _____

☐ Chucked It

(Fill in the blank with your own topic.)

1. _____

2. _____

3. _____

4. _____

5. _____

6. _____

7. _____

8. _____

9. _____

10. _____

☐ Chucked It

(Fill in the blank with your own topic.)

1. _____

2. _____

3. _____

4. _____

5. _____

6. _____

7. _____

8. _____

9. _____

10. _____

☐ Chucked It

CHUCK IT.